# Safe Houses I Have Known

## Also by Steve Healey

*10 Mississippi*
*Earthling*

# Safe

## Houses

### I    Have

#### Known

Steve Healey

**COFFEE HOUSE PRESS**
Minneapolis
2019

Coffee House Press books are available to the trade through our primary distributor, Consortium Book Sales & Distribution, cbsd.com or (800) 283-3572. For personal orders, catalogs, or other information, write to info@coffeehousepress.org.

Coffee House Press is a nonprofit literary publishing house. Support from private foundations, corporate giving programs, government programs, and generous individuals helps make the publication of our books possible. We gratefully acknowledge their support in detail in the back of this book.

LIBRARY OF CONGRESS CATALOGING-IN-PUBLICATION DATA

Names: Healey, Steve, 1966– author.
Title: Safe houses I have known / Steve Healey.
Description: Minneapolis : Coffee House Press, [2019]
Identifiers: LCCN 2019002957 (print) | LCCN 2019005435 (ebook) | ISBN
   9781566895699 (ebook) | ISBN 9781566895613 (trade pbk.)
Classification: LCC PS3608.E238 (ebook) | LCC PS3608.E238 A6 2019 (print) |
   DDC 811/.6—dc23
LC record available at https://lccn.loc.gov/2019002957

PRINTED IN THE UNITED STATES OF AMERICA

26 25 24 23 22 21 20 19    1 2 3 4 5 6 7 8

for my mother


and for my father,
who told me that if he ever wrote a memoir,
he'd call it *Safe Houses I Have Known*

# Contents

**3)**

**4)**

Safe Houses I Have Known

# 1

# If You Are a Spy

it's possible to keep a secret
sneak a piece of candy every minute

of the day for example keep a bag of M&M's
hidden nearby or really listen

to music like a cryptographer
sucking blood from a mysterious word

my daughter's word for music
is *munitz* if that's the way to spell it

she keeps saying it until I turn it on
"My Bonnie Lies over the Ocean" is another song

that eludes me I'm not used to the feel
of saltwater sloshing in my ears

it's true that when my father spied for the CIA
his cover name sounded fake

it was Victor T. Redvane I just failed to keep
that secret there's no need

to pretend a counterrevolution really came
and my body still lies over the Bay

of Pigs it's hard to know if a threat is real
inside the shell of my daughter's ear

a tick recently bit the soft skin
I tweezed the tick and put it in

a jar as evidence just in case
we were watched from outer space

# Do You Feel Safe at Home?

This is what the nurse asks me.
I'm wearing socks and a hospital gown.
Soon she'll walk me down a long hallway toward my procedure.
Outside it's snowing—everything's soft and shiny.

What does the word "safe" mean to you?
There once was a time when I drew pictures of hallways
that kept going around and around.
One hallway led to our kitchen—
all the special sharp knives I wasn't allowed to touch
stood on the counter and took a bow.

Do you feel comfortable in your body?
There once was a bird whose name was "word"
and each time I came near
it fluttered a little farther away.

On a scale from one to ten, how empty do you feel?
I became skilled at shoplifting.
I'd fill my pockets then bring a pack of gum to the cashier.
I'd look into his eyes and say, "Just this, please."

Do you ever lie in bed and pretend to be asleep?
The anesthesiologist says it's supposed to keep snowing
as he injects something milky into my IV.

Do you ever pretend to listen to what someone is saying?
There's so much that can be predicted.
A song I've been hearing for a long time.
I've got the whole world in my hands.
I've got all the angels in a jar, like pickles.
The jar is the size of the whole world.
I will love pickles till the day I die.
A parade is always going by.

Do you have any questions?

# Rearview

We almost accidentally ran over a little boy in the parking lot.
We hadn't expected anything terrible to almost happen while backing out.
It was a nice day, and we'd just had a nice time at the lake when

we almost accidentally ran over a little boy in the parking lot.
The radio was on, and we weren't paying attention while we backed out.
On the radio someone said the plan to raise taxes was dead in the water.

It was a nice day, and we'd just had a nice time at the lake when
we heard a little boy make the sound of almost being run over by a car.
There was a long moment of not understanding anything because

on the radio someone said the plan to raise taxes was dead in the water,
but then we looked and saw the little boy and began to understand.
He ran to his parents and they yelled at him for being careless.

There was a long moment of not understanding anything because
he was already so scared, then his face fell apart and he cried.
It happened in the United States in a terrible parking lot where

he ran to his parents and they yelled at him for being careless.
We began to drive again, we couldn't imagine doing anything else,
and we wanted to drive into the future and try not remembering that

it happened in the United States in a terrible parking lot where
we easily could have killed a little boy with our new eco-friendly car.
The sound of fender hitting his torso, his head hitting pavement,

and we wanted to drive into the future and try not remembering that
we'd had such a nice time floating in the water like dead people,
and we lived in a country of saying good-bye to something scary,

the sound of fender hitting torso, head hitting pavement.

# House of Helicopters

your own dusted-over father whispering—
*I'm sorry I'm sorry I'm sorry I'm sorry I'm sorry . . .*
—Sarah Fox, "Essay on My Memory"

the telephone was ringing again
I was watching a *M\*A\*S\*H* rerun

again and the telephone kept ringing
it was my dad calling again to ask

my mom why she was destroying
his life because she wanted a divorce

lying on the couch I watched Radar
yelling "choppers!" again while

helicopters delivered too many people
bleeding badly in the Korean War

my dad had almost been sent to fight
in Korea but instead the CIA hired him

to be a spy so he didn't have to bleed
in a war but eventually he'd call and

ask my mom why she was destroying
his life until she couldn't listen anymore

she'd hang up and he'd call back and
she'd tell me "just let it ring" and

I wouldn't move while Radar yelled
"choppers!" in the Korean War again

I wanted to apologize to the telephone
for having to keep ringing while I

watched another rerun of another
war no one understood and I wanted

to apologize to the M*A*S*H 4077th
for having to get bloody trying

to save too many people bleeding
for no good reason except my need

to watch something while I listened
to the telephone ringing again

I wanted to tell my dad I was sorry
that his life was being destroyed and

I wanted to tell my mom I was sorry
that my dad kept asking her why

she was destroying his life
this went on for so long eventually

I couldn't feel my body anymore
there was a war going on

I was trying not to be a problem
I lay very still on the couch while

Radar yelled "choppers!" and
the telephone rang again and again

# A State of Permanent Visibility

> The seeing machine . . . has become a transparent building in which
> the exercise of power may be supervised by society as a whole.
>
> —Michel Foucault, *Discipline & Punish*

Each street led to another street.
If we wanted, we could just keep going.
Some of us drove cars. Some walked.
It was amazing. Blood flowed under our skin.
Our eyelids blinked every few seconds.

Everyone was doing something with their bodies.
Some prayed. Some played cards.
The King of Hearts was showing,
but only the upper half of his body.
Our history was full of bodies that were so beautiful,
we wanted to be them or hurt them.

Our history was full of beautiful clothing
that hurt our bodies. We could buy this clothing
in stores. We could see mannequins in windows
wearing this clothing as if it didn't hurt.

Those mannequins were so still and perfect,
it was hard to believe. They all wanted to be
the Venus de Milo, who was so beautiful
her arms had been broken off and thrown away.
We all wanted to hold Venus de Milo
in our hands like an apple, because
she had held an apple back when she had hands.

We'd already eaten Marilyn Monroe like
a soft-serve ice cream cone until there was nothing
left of her. That's what we knew how to do.

We knew how to extinguish a star
and wash our hands and put ourselves to bed
night after night, and some of us were able to sleep.

One morning we woke and found
that we'd survived. We were older,
and we were breathing. Blood flowed
through our vessels. Our eyelids blinked.

We were hungry—in fact, we were famished.
Our children brought us poison soup
and we gulped it down. It was amazing.

# Central Intelligence

I spy with my little eye
my father the spy not looking like a spy.

Here we are in beautiful Langley,
home of the CIA, where nothing

happens. During the Cold War,
things not happening is normal.

I spy my father, who looks nothing
like a spy in his normal suit, smoking

normal cigarettes all day.
I spy with my little eye is a game

for my family to play in the car
on drives that go very far

because nothing happens when we go
nowhere except being unknown.

Here we are in beautiful metonymy
where "CIA" is concealed by "Langley,"

and if you've maintained anonymity,
you know there's so much not to see.

My family's dreams were classified.
If you've ever felt like a spy

in your own dream, then you know
nothing happens when you stay home.

Those who maintain anonymity
for the CIA call it "the agency,"

or even blander, "the company."
My father has a story about a story

no one is allowed to tell
while smoking normal cigarettes.

During the Cold War, it's normal
to notice that no Third World War

is happening, nothing remarkable.
I check in a mirror how little

and unremarkable my eye is.
It looks a lot like his.

# CIA Training Manual: Interrogation

effectiveness

depends upon

unsettling effect

the interrogation situation

in itself

disturbing to most people

the aim

to enhance this

disrupt radically

the familiar

there is an interval

of suspended animation

psychological

paralysis

a traumatic or sub-traumatic

which explodes

as it were

the world

his image of himself

the techniques that follow

intensified by

rapid exploitation

the moment of shock

## Fantasy Team

Behind every friendly face is another face
that looks at your face
with suspicion. A friendly work environment
requires the existence of
death. There's a school of architecture
that doesn't believe in entrances,
only exits. The function of
a lighthouse is to remind us that it used to
have a function. It's possible
to show all history with one
click, then clear history with another
click. Are you sure you want
to clear history? Seeing
the past requires a kind of subtraction.
An American dollar's eye
sees another eye that's not
there. Nor does this product contain
anything artificial or
natural; that's a promise.
This horse has no legs
because there never has been anywhere
to go. Because blue-sky thinking
requires the existence of
death, and death means
a warm front coming in.
That's why God made the idea of
God. And when it starts to rain,
when the new promises come
down like rain to wash away the old ones,
no need to pick up where
you left off. You're already reading
the next page in the semidark.
Your fantasy team will never be better
than your ability to fantasize,
and when you finally fall asleep,
they'll creep out of you
and let the Greek army into your home.

## Winter Panopticon

this window is for
looking at the blizzard
it helps me feel inside
while looking at the very busy snow

and the tree full of crows
who flap and caw
with their worried blizzardy minds

lately it's like all my friends' fathers
are dying and the hard part is
that we're old enough now
to feel like we should save them

or help them die peacefully
both of which are impossible

usually it's cancer cells that refuse
to stop growing but lately
it's everyone's heart that no longer
wants to pump blood unlike

this window that so effectively does
what it's supposed to do
i.e. look at the blizzard with crows in it
yet there is so much of this blizzard
the window can't see

I think of a print by Hiroshige
and how the whole scene rests
on the shoulders of a cat crouched
on a windowsill gazing
at the vast rice fields

many very tiny people are out there
gathered at a festival so far away
they're almost not there at all

what's left is us looking
at the cat's looking

and in the farthest distance
one lonely fabulous mountain
marking some outer edge of earth

and beyond that the beginning
of not-earth burning orange
where the sun has just set

Hiroshige was an artist
and also a firefighter
assigned to protect Edo Castle
a position his father passed on to him
and then he passed on to his son

just before dying he wrote
*I leave my brush in the East*
*and set forth on my journey*

I think Hiroshige
would have liked this window
with its snowy ghosts

I think the fathers
have not quite died yet
they've gathered like crows
to worry about the weather

# A Map of Our Imperial Body

The problem is that our territory keeps
growing. North grows south.

Skin stretches over ocean.
Where did all these miles come from?

Ever since we dropped Fat Man
on Nagasaki. Now we say

"obesity epidemic." Still, a spoonful
of sugar helps the empire go

down. How about some Rocky Road
and Zoloft? Watch *Finding Nemo*

again to numb the fear of being
relocated across the planet?

Side effects may include dizziness
and nausea. Occasional loss

of ability to ignore the loss
of someone else's mother tongue or

half their face. Plus, we've lost
our keys, and logic doesn't find them.

Some places are so obvious
we can't get there. In a jacket pocket

on our dozing body in an airplane
at ten thousand feet. Thank God

for imperial measurement.
To be more useful, maps may be

deliberately inaccurate. Maps use
scale to consume more inches

of the earth. Borders are useful
for circulating blood back to the heart

or spilling it on breaking news.
Thank God for helping us clean up

the mess. Let's put our hands
together and pray like hell we're not

sent on another secret mission.
The king will see us now, but

never look him in the eye.
Some things the king should never

be told. Like the story about how
God lays an egg. Or the world is

an egg, and we're getting hungrier.
Or we're playing egg toss,

taking another step back each time
we catch the egg. In theory,

we keep expanding the empire
until the egg breaks.

## Spy vs. Spy Haiku

Two clouds parted by a
mountain. Two spies view each other
through binoculars.

—

What will morning choose:
dagger umbrella, rocket plunger,
bomb cake, or ray-gun glove?

—

Spring rain. Everything is shiny.
A spy hides behind lilacs, holding
a bucket of poison.

—

If you've ever dreamed of
a locked safe marked "top secret,"
it wasn't a dream.

# CIA Training Manual: The Art of Deception

here are instructions

so little generally is known

because successful deception

"already in the mind"

does not fool the eye but

the trick is merely

added to other actions        not noticed

the trickster

salts his food

salt openly goes into

left hand

hand is dropped        calls no attention

naturalness in performance

trickery

is a lie acted

but all actions

which are surprising

immediately

forgotten        by        rational

for instance

pouring a beverage

over the food

not remembered if        seems accidental

body        twitched        in pain

"there must be a pin

on the chair"

all the stronger if

a pin is produced

a simple explanation

# In Junior High School

I sat in the classroom listening
to the clock. I didn't say
anything. I touched my lips
too much. I listened to the wind
rubbing against the windows.
The field behind my school
sometimes disappeared
under snow. One night my father
told me that he was a spy
for the CIA. He said that being
a spy was like James Bond
but less exciting. He said
I should never tell anyone
he was a spy. If anyone asked
I should say he worked for
the State Department. I listened
to my father but didn't say
anything. I forgot I was there.
It was dark outside. After
that night I went on being
a student in junior high school.
I sat in the classroom and
didn't tell anyone my father
was a spy for the CIA.
I forgot there were windows
between me and the field of snow.
My history teacher showed us
a bar graph of Soviet missiles.
They were towering over
the American missiles. He said
we were losing the Cold War.
I looked outside. I could see
footsteps in the field of snow.
I didn't say anything.

2

# Choose Your Life

Either an intruder's in the house
or I'm shopping online.
An intruder or stargazer lilies
in a vase. A noise my body makes.
My body in a different room.
Yesterday we played I was
the prisoner. I ate the toy bread.
I tried to remember a song.
A song about a train we keep
missing. A noise the windows
make. Either burnt sienna
or terra-cotta curtains. Either
I forgot my password or
the name of the street I grew up on.
I grew up thinking my clothes
were shrinking. I sang
*this train is bound for glory.*
I stole cigarettes from my father
while he slept. I prayed
for something terrible to happen.
What was the name of the hurricane
that shattered our windows?
Either it *just happened* or
we deserved it. Never enough time
to evacuate. Ready to check out?
The sun's still there behind
the clouds. My body still
bound for glory. That grackle
flying into the mirror again
and again, or laundry
waiting in a basket.

# Do You Remember Being Clandestine?

before this morning's rain fell in lines
slanting not quite the same direction

before this poem tried to speak to you
not quite on the anniversary of your death

but close enough for government work
I mean when did you start to self-destruct

so many years erasing your vital organs
before divulging your government work

to me I mean what does a CIA case officer
really do gathering "human intelligence"

recruiting "assets" maybe paying off
a janitor or bureaucrat to pass you

a classified document as Mom passed
my tiny body into the sterile hands

of the obstetrician but of course not before
you first met her in the Berlin CIA base

just after the Berlin Wall went up either
to keep people in or out alive or dead

before King Kong destroyed Godzilla
before we sang I'd like to teach the world

to drink way too much Coke before
inventing covert operations to destroy

other people less obviously no we didn't
want to see the dead bloody bodies

anymore we wanted the rain to wash it
all away we wanted to stop believing

in ghosts but then you came back
to sit with me in this house wearing

your nice coffin suit well they
cleaned you up pretty well didn't they

I guess it's too late to be clandestine
do you remember being afraid

I guess it's too late to be afraid
do you remember being alive

# CIA Training Manual: Theory of Coercion

to exploit          internal conflicts

                                        wrestle with himself
                    also
        superior outside force
                        upon the subject's resistance

                                                loss of
defenses          acquired by          civilized man

                    homeostatic derangement
                                        anxiety
                most people
                            will talk
    moral objection to

                irreversible          damage
                                    exceeds the scope
of this paper
                    what is fully clear          however

        coercive manipulation
    may impair
                    fine distinction          not

        ability to answer
                        gross questions
                                        "Are you a
Soviet agent?"


            is not a game

# Coin Toss at Dusk

Anyway, the coin you tossed is still in the air . . .

—Valerie Mejer Caso, "I Just Realized"

if you could gather
all the neighborhood moms and dads
including yours
onto the head of a nickel

all their little feet pressing down
on Thomas Jefferson's perfect face
while the coin balanced on your thumbnail
waits to be flipped

the parents look a bit nervous
as your thumb pops up
and sends the nickel somersaulting toward the sky
it may be pure chance
that determines the outcome

heads up the parents live
tails up they're crushed by beautiful Monticello
and all the neighborhood kids will be orphans
free to stay up all night
and do whatever the hell they please

but if you could hold your breath
and pause the coin's journey in midair
as Jefferson once held his breath
until he thought of the next word to write down

you squint your eyes just right as the sun sets
and see yourself in the future
giving birth to a bright-orange gumball

a black hole surrounded by all your cavity teeth
fifty stars floating on an amniotic sea

certain unalienable rights
and a permanent war with aliens

dead grass
long shadows
shiny windows

a human baby with only one brain

something to buy with a nickel

before the mosquitoes come out
and your parents call you inside

and you breathe

# Spectral Evidence

The past stays in the past unless you
think about it. Before diving into water

my dad made the sign of the cross.
He was born in Salem sometime after

the witch trials. When I was a kid,
I wanted to be a witch. But I worried

that other people would be afraid of me.
Witches are only ugly if you're afraid

of them. There are many ways to ignore
what you want. There are many ways

to ignore your biological needs.
In medieval Europe, you were a witch

if you floated in water. As a kid,
I spent a lot of time floating in water.

I spent a lot of time alone in bathrooms.
Sometimes I put blush on my cheeks.

In church, I made a sign of the cross.
As a kid, my dad watched a lot of

horror movies at the local theater.
Horror movies get smaller and sadder

as the years go by. Coming soon:
another spectacular way to die.

Coming soon: all the tears of the past.
In Salem, you could be accused of

afflicting someone with an apparition.
In Salem, nineteen people were hanged

for being witches. Incantations make
the planet rotate every twenty-four hours.

In school, I learned to cast a spell
on myself. I learned to write my own

obituary. School policy prohibited
my blushing cheeks. We took a field trip

to the bottomless swimming pool.
There's a right way and a wrong way

to be baptized. Witches float because
they're made of water. We took

a field trip to the execution museum.
I wrote my dad's obituary with my eyes

closed. I dove into the deep end
with my hands tied behind my back.

# Civilization

this morning I pay $109 to have my cat killed
because he's almost dead
I hold him in the sterile room crying and crying
until someone comes with the syringe

later I'm still a monster
and upon that monster it cries and cries a motherlode of snow
and I disappear until the spring melt
the alarm clock turns green because it's time to wake up

all the trees making green plans
all the bodies becoming soil
all fifty-six ongoing armed conflicts around the planet
the planet seen from outer space

but now all I can see is this monster poem
this poem witnessing its own monstrosity
as the spring sun comes closer
conjuring baby-green leaves from their buds

my daughter wants to glue glitter to everything
or cut everything up with scissors

marshmallow clouds sailing over the recycling plant
the sad red van parked near the group home on Selby
selling drugs to the recovering drug addicts

the IMAX movie about a single breath
the one breath ever breathed
the hole in which we placed the cardboard box
in which we placed our dead cat

later in the dark I sing "Amazing Grace"
my daughter so close to sleep
the streetlight in the alley turns on

# Spy vs. Spy Haiku

Sun setting. A spy slingshots
a stick of dynamite over the wall.
It bounces back, fuse still lit.

—

Open the codebook.
Random numbers rise off the page.
Dandelion seeds in the wind.

—

Summer solstice. All night
sleeping under a teetering anvil—
dawn comes too late.

# Invisible Civil War

Someone I once threatened to kill recently killed himself.
We grew up in the same neighborhood called "Stonewall Manor."
I wish I were making this up, but I'm not. It's really true that

someone I once threatened to kill recently killed himself.
His name was Greg, and as a kid he wore corrective leg braces.
I remember he was often nervous and spoke with a stutter.

I wish I were making this up, but I'm not. It's really true that
I threatened to kill him if he didn't sponsor me for a charity walk.
I must have needed an easy way to forget my own pain by

threatening someone who was nervous and spoke with a stutter.
I must have also been trying to impress my friend Brad.
A few years earlier, Brad's mom had died of kidney failure.

I must have needed an easy way to forget my own pain by
adding more pain to the nice green lawns of Stonewall Manor.
Although Brad lived across the street, we never talked about

the pain he must have felt when his mom died of kidney failure.
Our neighborhood was named after "Stonewall" Jackson,
the Confederate general known for killing many Union soldiers.

Although Brad lived across the street, we never talked about
Amy next door, who died after being hit by a delivery truck,
or any of the ghosts haunting our scared white subdivision.

A Confederate general known for killing many Union soldiers,
Jackson died after being accidentally shot by one of his own.
Growing up, I didn't see the civil war that was all around us,

or any of the ghosts haunting our scared white subdivision.
When my parents found out that I threatened to kill Greg,
they were already separated and in the process of divorcing.

Growing up, I didn't see the civil war that was all around us,
but that night when they took me to Greg's house to apologize,
I knew my parents were angry in a deeply frightened way.

They were already separated and in the process of divorcing,
and they must've suddenly felt the pain we never talked about.
For a while it seemed like there wasn't enough air to breathe.

I knew my parents were angry in a deeply frightened way
because what I'd done had revealed how broken we were.
After I heard recently that Greg committed suicide,

it seemed for a while like there wasn't enough air to breathe.
A few years ago Greg contacted me and we reconnected,
although we never mentioned that I once threatened to kill him.

After I heard recently that Greg committed suicide,
I recalled how we'd talked about our old neighborhood,
and how he'd sent me his music and I'd sent him my poetry,

although we never mentioned that I once threatened to kill him.

# Rules of the Game

Everyone is a suspect.
Everyone is Colonel Mustard.

Colonel Mustard in the basement
with a toothpick. Everywhere

is a crime scene, everything
a weapon. Following the rules

is the most dangerous weapon.
Players must identify the murderer

by looking at each other's faces.
If you have to ask, you're already

dead. Remember not to breathe.
The question worth asking should

not be asked. Every word counts.
Every suspect has nothing to say.

Every breath is your last penny.
Also, past performance does not

guarantee future respiration.
One afternoon walking home

from school you find a dollar on
the sidewalk. George Washington

stares at you with his dead face.
One morning delivering newspapers

you see a dead body in a parked car.
You feel guilty but didn't commit

the crime. One summer at camp
you learn to follow the rules

by hiding your sadness. Now
the player to the left must visualize

your corpse. You are accused
of everything. Now your body is

covered in shadows or bruises.
You have the right to remain silent.

Each player takes a deep breath
and holds it. Each player must die

trying to win. The game is over
when no one wins. Everyone dies.

# Brainwashing

Here is a broken time machine.
Here a broken head. A star in the sky
controls my thoughts. My thoughts move
too slowly. Tonight Dad's home
from his job as a spy in time
to give me a bath. His fingers lather
No More Tears shampoo into my hair,
a cigarette dangling from his lips,
his eyes squinting through curlicues
of smoke. Here is the spit on my tongue.
I can't control my bodily fluids.
I don't know he's a spy yet. I don't
have any tears. I have an ocean
and a small blue boat. I have Geppetto
trapped in the belly of a whale.
I have hell in the belly of Geppetto.
Here is an Atomic Fireball
to force open the whale's mouth.
When you wish upon the lips that decide
whether you live or die. When
something terrible falls from the sky
into our yard. Here is the one dandelion
that survived all the weed killer
we sprayed. Here the ghosts
of its dead family. Tomorrow
I'll wake in my bed in my own urine.
I can't control my bodily fluids.
Tomorrow at school I'll get
another nosebleed, bright-red drop
landing on my notebook. My thoughts—
they move too slowly. Now
is the time to see no more ghosts.
Cover up the mirrors and stop
the clocks. Eeny meeny
miney moe, my body clean
from head to toe.

# CIA Training Manual:
## Non-coercive Interrogation Techniques

### THE ALL-SEEING EYE

                                  skilled manipulation

        can convince a naive

                                      all his secrets are out

### THE INFORMER

        tricks possible

                        hidden microphone he "found"

              in whispers

### JOINT SUSPECTS

                                knowing grin

                  "we'll get to you"

      in A's mind B is talking

### IVAN IS A DOPE

                      cover story was ill-contrived

personalize this pitch

                  his true friend

JOINT INTERROGATORS

"shut up!
I've broken crumb-bums
I'll break this one wide open"


SPINOZA AND MORTIMER SNERD

complaints that
even the stupidest men

punishment for "don't know"


A WOLF IN SHEEP'S CLOTHING

staged "escape"
by a stool pigeon

not recommended


ALICE IN WONDERLAND

obliterate the familiar
replace it with the weird

eerie meaninglessness


REGRESSION

retarding and advancing clocks

days and nights are jumbled
until he is no longer able

## Covert Ghazal

All the leaves are brown, but a few have not yet
fallen. A few have not tasted the ground, and yet

it is late fall, very late. Don't get me wrong,
there is a lot of bareness out there, but I will not yet

let my tongue say that the bareness is total.
You say this fall I'm more open to being tasted, yet

I think what you mean is that still a small part
of me is closed. In my mouth a little green mint, as yet

undissolved, waits for next spring when all
the leaf buds will burst hugely into green yet

again. Still, at this brown autumnal moment
I'm breathing with anticipation like a leaf as yet

unfallen who does not want to let go, because now
I'm finally afraid enough not to fall, and yet

my hand can almost taste the ground. Almost,
for what I really want is to turn this page that's not yet

ready to turn, to leave this leaflike page behind,
because I want the next page, the painful yet

tasty anticipation of my fingers touching your lips
to read all the words that you've almost said, and yet

you are all the me I've wanted to be, because
when I ask if you're ready, you say "not yet"

# Mysterious Bruise

Do I know how this bruise came to be on my arm?
I do not. More precisely, although I know that a bruise
is caused by damaged capillaries leaking blood
into the interstitial tissue under the skin,
said capillary damage is usually caused by
external trauma, like a punch from a fist,
and I have zero memory of receiving such a blow.

Nonetheless, the bruise does exist, and because
it has the exact size and oval shape of a robin's egg,
I've lately been haunted by my late grandmother's voice
warning me as a child that a robin will peck my eyes out
if I ever touch its egg. As you might expect,
I developed an irrational yet very real fear
of robins and pretty much all avifauna.

Which makes my residence in this tower all the more
unexpected. While my ornithophobia has never
been more intense, nestled up here I do feel
more birdlike than ever before, as if I
have now become the very thing that I fear.

A further complication is that this tower
is a former water tower refurbished for human occupancy.
Thus, although I'm suspended 115 feet above ground,
it's impossible not to feel that I'm floating
in a great cylinder of water—24,500 gallons of water
to be precise. The water that once occupied this space,
in other words, occupies it now as a ghostly presence.

Perhaps this explains why I've been so thirsty.
Besides that spectral water, the only factual water
in this tower is that which I keep pouring
into the water glass standing on my table
like a small commemorative tower honoring
the larger tower that contains it.

And as I pour water into my body
I see my face reflected in the bottom of the glass.
Except that I don't quite recognize myself,
as if I were that person at a reception whose name
I don't quite remember, and I'm not wearing a name tag.
Or I *am* wearing a name tag but it's blank,
it just says, "Hello, my name is."
Or my face suddenly looks very old,
my eyes are dim like distant stars.
Or my eyes are not there at all.

3

## My Father's Knees

Wherever you feel discomfort in the body,
make yourself at home. A knee without cartilage

is your creaking cradle. Notice where
discomfort ends and pain begins.

There's a special pill that takes me home.
What I love about the new year is how

it comes in easy-to-swallow caplets.
Last night we talked about steaming lobsters alive

for the new year. What I love about sacrifice
is not doing it myself. My father once

stood on the deck of a ship that was sinking
in the English Channel. Dying is easy.

The desire to be at ease is killing me.
Shakespeare knew how to kill his way

out of a scene. Could you please press PAUSE?
I have to find Dover. I have cultivated

a certain helplessness. I cannot fix the teleporter
without your help. Currently we're unable

to transfer matter without traversing space.
Wherever you lay your headache is

the right dosage. Dover is where your pain
hopes to end. If only I had an energy drink.

Thank God, a natural disaster to make things
interesting. Up next, the year in extreme weather.

Indeed, the heath is insane tonight.
Could you please press THE SIXTEENTH CENTURY?

That was a good one for pain. Since then
much has come into view. My shadow stretched

so long I updated my status. I cultivated
a certain newness. Last night we talked about

inventing a new word. And I want to be there
when we get there. Welcome back to the year in

obfuscation. Stay tuned for the year's best
neologisms. Thanks for making everything

a competition. Thanks for the terrible conflicts.
Reading is the new terrorism. Once my father

read a play that was four centuries old.
For the new year I resolve to become fluent in

English. From my father I inherited English
and a lack of cartilage in my right knee.

For the next thirty seconds the new year will be
painless. I have nowhere to go.

## How About

the house is haunted but
all the ghosts are nice ones
mostly nice but sometimes mean
when they eat our snacks without asking
how about there's a ghost horse
with big snack lips but she's nice and gives us
slow-gallop rides over furniture hills

all the ghosts are part of our family
but grown-ups can't see them
how about I'm the daughter you're the son
or we're both half daughter half son
half comet half horse
going around the carousel

over there is the black hole where
we ate crackers and grapes today for snack
in that corner all the galaxies
that don't care if we don't
say please and thank you

how about Dad never says we have to clean up
this mess because he's our tiny cute baby
he's always napping in his crib
or he's in the room where he writes poems
and inside him there's a baby who has
another baby inside him

how about the babies have a war
inside him and become orphans or
how about we're the orphans in a poem
Dad writes then we're adopted
by the ghost horse and off
we ride through the snowy air
we say the words
and disappear

# I Can't Say This to You

excuse me while I procrastinate
a little more before beginning this poem

to you while I fold laundry while
a concealed camera moon watches me

through the living room window folding
my elbows and knees into neat stacks

of body while eyeing the moon cookie
waiting on a plate for me to eat it or

I watch the grainy televised summer
of '69 moon landing I don't remember

watching as a one-small-step toddler but
you told me we watched while living

in Vienna where you were stationed as
a CIA spy you also told me I once snuck

into the Vienna night in my pajamas while
you walked our dog and had a smoke

like dads did I did try to follow you
and of course spy on you but I got lost

and scared even if I could see above me
that same moon until finally some nice

police picked me up and I wouldn't speak
even in English much less German

but somehow they helped me get home
and my little lost white American body

was of course always safe while the planet
kept rotating while others we saw as

others on the planet kept dying while
we kept not looking too closely while

the CIA was secretly killing thousands
of others in Vietnam while I slept in

our house under a clear Vienna sky and
even years later never really asked you

what you knew or what you could say
you knew to me or to yourself or what

knowing felt like while the moon lit
the edges of everyone who had a body

## CIA Museum

### INSECTOTHOPTER

                                 first flight
     insect-sized vehicle
                                            to prove
                intelligence
                           miniature engine
to move       wings
                 control
                         too
difficult

### MODIFIED LADY'S MAKEUP COMPACT

          symbols represent
      words
                       concealed
inside the mirror
           by tilting
               is revealed

### BODYWORN SURVEILLANCE EQUIPMENT

       what is         appearance

          nothing at all

walking to buy a newspaper

                       drizzly day
       miniature camera
            behind
    button

## CALTROP (TIRE SPIKE)

                              simplest weapon
we ever
                    whatever

          punctured or injured
                              scattered onto enemy
roadways or

          medieval knights on horseback


## PIGEON CAMERA

                    light
                                        strapped to
its breast
                    would         fly over

          concealed
                              among thousands
of other birds


## "ATTITUDE" HAT

                              CIA officer wore

          Salvadoran Civil War
                                        days when
things were not going well

                                    improving
                    less and less

## "DEAD DROP" SPIKE

one person

       other person

             prearranged

location

       one could push

into the ground


## MICRODOT CAMERA

         the Cold War

     relied on

  a tiny piece of film

        period at the end

of this sentence

# Subliminal Advertisement

I'd walk a mile for a Camel.
Moreover, said Thoreau,
you must walk like a camel.
Therefore, with four crooked legs
I'd walk a crooked mile across an Egyptian desert.
I'd saunter like a furry comma
through the Mall of America,
elevating my heart rate for twenty minutes.
I'd haul my humps all the way to Glocca Morra
if waiting for me at the finish line were
a tasty factory-made cigarette.

In addition, it is said that Jesus said
that it's easier for a camel to pass through
a needle's eye than for a crooked man
to enter the kingdom of Glocca Morra.
It's also said that camels store water in their humps,
but that's not true. Over time
they've adapted to long journeys with little water.
They retain it in their kidneys and intestines
so efficiently—their urine is thick syrup,
their feces dry enough to fuel fires.

Furthermore, according to Thoreau,
camels are the only beasts who ruminate while
walking. They eat, then regurgitate
what they eat, then chew what they regurgitate
to enjoy it again, all the while
walking a mile through their crooked thoughts.
Camels, in other words, are thoughtful vehicles,
and according to Jesus, they're the only beast
to have replaced the wheel where it
had already been established prior to the invention
of the internal combustion engine.

Thus, they're ideal for the Second Coming,
and when they finally cross the finish line
and swallow that cud, it's time
to have a Camel and walk no more
crooked miles. The fires of Glocca Morra
are ready to touch my lips.

# Villanelle on Blood

I cut myself to see what's inside my body.
I hid the razor blade under a rock outside.
*It was an accident,* I told the people who love me.

I saw my blood drip on the red bedsheets
like an animal who uses camouflage to lie.
I cut myself to remove the dirty part of my body,

but I was surprised by how much I could bleed.
My wound gushed a dark night of starlight.
It was an accident, agreed the people who love me,

but in their eyes I saw they didn't believe.
A moth appears to be the rock on which it alights.
I cut myself to forget the shape of my body

and remember how ketchup looked so tidy
when I spread it on a hamburger with a knife.
If there were an accident, how scary to see me

with blade in my flesh, red pouring on the meat,
my parents coming to save me before I die.
I cut myself to open a mouth on my body.
It was an accident, but I could finally breathe.

## Surveillance Video of a Bridge

This is what a bridge looks like.
This is a bridge crossing a river on a planet
orbiting a sun. This is a structure

providing passage over a physical obstacle
such as a river on a planet once upon
a time. What being in a vehicle

crossing a bridge looks like upon a time.
This is a vehicle that looks like
many vehicles shiny in the light
of the sun, moving across a structure

that looks like a perfect horizontal strip
of land across nothing but air.
This is a person who once upon
a 6:04 p.m. on a Wednesday in August

thinks nothing about what gravity
looks like 115 feet above
an actual river. What people look like

in vehicles wearing sunglasses,
remembering chicken salad for lunch,
listening to news about a war
happening somewhere—people killing
other people. This is in fact what

a bridge seen by a security camera
on a Wednesday in August at 6:04 p.m.,
the shiny vehicles, the planet turning
away from the sun, the sun falling
in the sky toward evening, looks like.

In fact, the bridge begins to fall
at 6:05 p.m. It drops quickly, in fact,
under the force of gravity. In fact,

this is what 115 feet looks like.
The bridge and the vehicles on the bridge
and the people in the vehicles and
the sunglasses on the people.

This is what falling looks like.

This is what afraid. This is what my God.
This is what no bridge, in fact,

the absence of bridge. Once upon a time,
in fact. What nothing looks like.

This is absence seen by a security camera
at 6:06 p.m. on a Wednesday.

What, in fact. In fact, this.

## Spy vs. Spy Haiku

At dusk, a mosquito penetrates
a safe house. The crescent moon
wants to come in too.

—

Bombs shaped like dolls
parachute from a black helicopter.
Leaves let go of an oak tree.

—

Autumn lake. A spy in a rowboat
swallowed by a remote-control whale.
The surface grows still again.

## Please Forgive Me for Writing This Poem

My wife was vomiting, and I thought maybe I should help her.
Then I saw that she was trying to vomit on me as punishment for being bad,
but then to be less bad I thought I should be present and focus on the fact that

my wife was vomiting, and I thought maybe I should help her.
Actually I did have some digestive juices and pieces of meat on me,
and I thought about how earlier I should have washed the dinner dishes,

but then to be less bad I thought I should be present and focus on the fact that
I might be able to comfort my wife while she experienced the violent pain of
transferring meat from the inside of her body to the outside.

And I thought about how earlier I should have washed the dinner dishes
because my wife had made dinner, a delicious meat loaf made of ground beef
from a cow who never imagined how much pleasure she could give us by

transferring meat from the inside of her body to the outside,
meat that my wife then cooked and that we then put inside our bodies.
Later, a full moon poured light onto our bed when my wife let go of the meat

from a cow who never imagined how much pleasure she could give us by
becoming our delicious dinner. Selfishly I didn't do the dishes,
and selfishly I instead thought about writing a poem like this one.

Later, a full moon poured light onto our bed when my wife let go of the meat,
and because some of it got on my body, I thought she was punishing me.
As I rubbed her shoulders, part of me was afraid to really be there,

and selfishly I instead thought about writing a poem like this one.
But then it occurred to me that I could love my wife more than my fear,
and that there was no other place in the world right then, even though

as I rubbed her shoulders, part of me was afraid to really be there.

## Self-Surveillance

You're condemned to die.
You're condemned to photograph
your death. Your camera is light but
feels so heavy. You press the shutter button

and fall for the first time. You get up
and continue. You meet your mother.
You ask if she remembers when
you fell out of your crib. She says,

"Your father and I are getting a divorce."
She says "your father" as if he were
your problem now. You say,
"You already divorced him years ago."
She says, "Some things you never forget
how to do." You meet a man

named Simon. He helps you carry
the camera. You take a photo of yourselves.
You ask your mother if she remembers
when you fell out of that apple tree.
She says she'll call you later,
after she divorces your father.

A saint named Veronica wipes
your face. You photograph your new face
and fall a second time. A pattern of falling

has clearly been established.
You get up expecting that you'll soon
fall again. You're a forever faller.
A future Hall-of-Fame faller.

You meet the women of Jerusalem.
They say they'll do anything
for you. They'll sing about you.
You're famous. Your camera captures
everything. You fall a third time.

It's your best fall ever. You're
stripped and prepped for the end.

It's a beautiful evening. An amazing light
surrounds you. You die on your camera.

You're downloaded into the tomb,
then returned to the womb.

Everything seems possible.

# Overthrow Install

1)

in Iran CIA overthrows Prime Minister Mossadegh
in military coup and in Guatemala President Arbenz
overthrown in CIA-backed military coup and in the Congo
CIA overthrows and assassinates Prime Minister Lumumba
and President Bosch in the Dominican Republic
overthrown in military coup backed by CIA and in Ecuador
CIA overthrows President Arosemana in military coup
and CIA-supported military coup in Brazil overthrows
President Goulart and in South Vietnam President Diem
overthrown and assassinated in military coup supported
by CIA and in Indonesia CIA backs military coup
overthrowing President Sukarno and military coup backed
by CIA overthrows Prime Minister Kanellopoulos
in Greece and in Bolivia President Torres overthrown
in CIA-supported military coup and CIA overthrows
and assassinates President Allende in Chile and in Haiti
CIA backs military coup overthrowing President Aristide

2)

in Iran CIA installs shah of Iran who rules for decades with
brutal secret police and for decades in Guatemala CIA installs
series of ruthless right-wing dictators who kill thousands of people
and CIA-installed dictator Mobutu Sese Seko rules in the Congo
for decades with extreme cruelty and in the Dominican Republic
CIA installs repressive right-wing military junta and in Ecuador
CIA-installed military junta commits severe human rights abuses
and brutal military junta installed by CIA rules for decades
in Brazil with CIA-trained death squads and in South Vietnam
CIA installs military junta while U.S. dramatically increases
troops to fight against Viet Cong and in Indonesia CIA installs
General Suharto who massacres as many as a million civilians
accused of being communist and in Greece CIA-installed
military junta orders widespread torture and murder of opponents
and in Bolivia CIA installs dictator Hugo Banzer who oversees
the torture and murder of thousands of political opponents and
in Chile CIA installs General Pinochet who has thousands
of his own people tortured and murdered and in Haiti
military dictators installed by CIA brutalize the country as
thousands of refugees attempt to escape by boat and often die

# Disinformation

An ocean wave is energy moving across the water's surface.

A death rattle is the sound of air moving through saliva
that collects in a dying person's throat.

When I look at the ocean, a wave moves across it.
My father is dying of thirst.

Typically, a person dies within twenty-four hours
of the death rattle's onset.

When I turn to look at the bay, a great blue heron takes flight.
The sun turns pink and sinks behind the bay.

The problem with the world is that it's never pink enough.
I drink a pink drink that's never drink enough.

I open a cocktail umbrella, and a great blue heron takes flight
toward a sky that's never near enough.
I look at a pretzel and salivate.

Humans need salt to survive
but die if they drink ocean water because
it contains more salt than their kidneys can process.

There are never enough pretzels to eat.
The problem is that we think there's a problem.

A cubic foot of ocean water contains about 2.2 pounds of salt.

Even my father on the beach says he sees a ship having a problem.
My father on the ship says he sees a beach.
My father on the ship that is sinking.

The pink sun that sinks behind the bay.
The salt that tells me a lie.

## How I Become a Son

I watch your face telling me
your face covered with skin

I see the hairs you missed shaving
my face too young to shave

your eyes too old to be so moist
the smell of drinks on your lips

telling me what happened a few
years ago when we lived in Rome

when a woman we knew demanded
to talk to you in the embassy

you were called down to the lobby
you tell me she was very upset when

she told you what was happening
she said her husband and your wife

who was my mom were having
an "affair" was the word she told you

she wanted our family gone she'd
gone public with your CIA identity

she'd blown your cover to force us
to leave that's why Mom suddenly

took us kids back to the States why
you disappeared for a while since

you needed to disappear so they
sent you to the Cyprus CIA station

to occupy a desk after an "incident"
there you tell me they just needed

a body there to occupy a desk
so you sat all day in Cyprus

in a chair with a bullet hole in it
but what happened to the bullet

you didn't say you sat in a shot chair
passing time reading a pulp novel

from which you learned the word
"cuckold" was the word you tell me

for a husband like you whose wife
had an affair while your face is

covered with skin telling my face
which is there to be told but also

gone away already moved on
to not telling Mom tomorrow

what you'd just told me then
years of not telling her already

my skin-covered face looking
like it had nothing to tell

like underneath I was just
stardust and space

4

# Where My Poetry Comes From

I wrote a book of poems while living in
a federally designated superfund cleanup site.
All around me in the soil were lethal levels of arsenic.
I called the Environmental Protection Agency to ask
if my poetry would be okay. They said they did not
understand poetry but the threat of arsenic poisoning
was quite low. After the book was published,
critics argued that it contained lethal levels of arsenic.
I had tried to convince myself otherwise,
but now I do see arsenic in almost every line.

Where did it come from? The EPA's current theory
is that the chemical, scattered by winds around
my neighborhood, originated from a pesticide plant
that used to operate nearby. In fact, arsenic was once
commonly used in pesticides and other "-cides."
It was also once a popular tool for committing murder
because, prior to modern methods of arsenic detection,
its presence was difficult to trace in human bodies.
Interestingly, because the ruling classes valued
discreetness and potency when murdering one another,
arsenic has been called "the poison of kings."

One year my school's play was *Arsenic and Old Lace,*
but all I remember are a lot of murders and a kind
of Panama Canal graveyard in the basement.
It's possible that my arsenic poisoning began back
then, sitting for so long in the hard wooden seat
of that auditorium. It may be that my arsenic book
is really a summary of many years of bodily failures,
leading me inexorably to inhabit this superfund site.

Yesterday I watched the people in white suits
excavating a yard. One was leaning on a shovel,
smoking a cigarette, and as he exhaled I could see
his lips moving as if he were talking to himself.
I'm pretty sure he was reciting one of my poems.

# Identity Theft

I had a thought, after a poem written after
Catullus. After my cat named
Catullus. After I stole

all the thinking from ancient Rome.
I had a thought about how I lied about the name
of my cat. My cat's name is Dickinson,

and many thoughts have I
stolen from her. She's actually a deer

named Dickinson. I replaced her
with another deer fashioned after,
in the manner of, largely influenced by, working in
the Dickinsonian tradition of,
that original deer. After

Julie Andrews sang *doe, a deer,*
*a female deer,* I thought naming that deer after her
would be a good idea because
she brings us back to *doe, ray, me,*
*a name I call myself.* Me

thinking after the sun goes down a bit more brightly
the day after the winter solstice. After

my neighbor who survived cancer
told me about a neighbor just diagnosed with
cancer. You have to learn how to be

alive again. Even after
eating bad American Chinese food,
I tried to save my body with a fortune cookie:
*you might not die a scary death.* After

having a thought after myself,
after the end of my personality and person,
my sadness and hope. After

I made a decision—no more stealing
from the dead, not even
from the ancient Roman poet Catullus.

Because I decided to ignore that decision.
Because it was the morning after

my cat died, and I knew
I had never been original.

It was time for breakfast,
and I was ready to share my everything bagel

with everyone in the world.

## Safe Houses I Have Known

> Safe houses I have known, thought Guillam, looking round the gloomy flat. He could write of them the way a commercial traveller could write about hotels. . . .
>
> Either you are pretending you live there, or that you are adept anywhere; or simply that you think of everything. In the trade, naturalness is an art, Guillam decided.
>
> —John le Carré, *Tinker Tailor Soldier Spy*

I don't know much about the safe houses my father knew.
They kept his secrets safe while looking like other houses.
He looked like other dads, not like a spy for the CIA.

We lived in a suburban house when not stationed abroad.
When stationed in Rome I started to hear my parents fight.
Returning stateside my mom said she wanted a divorce.

In our suburban neighborhood all the houses looked alike.
Suddenly my dad no longer lived in our house with us.
He was not supposed to enter without permission.

My mom said she didn't love him. She wanted a divorce.
It seemed like the neighbors didn't notice he was missing.
We didn't know what to say to them about our family.

One day my dad entered the house without permission.
Opening the door without knocking, he came into the foyer.
He called out to us. It sounded like he was crying.

We didn't know what to say to him about his sadness.
We came into the foyer and stood there watching him.
He was crying. He was holding a kitchen knife in his hand.

He was crying and pleading with us to do something.
He was offering us the knife handle, asking us to stab him.
He said, "I can't do it myself. Will you please do it?"

He kept crying and holding the knife handle out to us.
I know we didn't stab him, and he didn't stab himself.
I don't remember anything else. He must have gone away.

I remember how he asked, "Will you please do it?"
We must have gone back to the family room to watch TV.
He must have gone away. I don't remember anything else.

# CIA Training Manual: A Study of Assassination

contrived accident is the most

causes little excitement

only casually investigated

efficient

fall of seventy-five feet or more

elevator shaft        windows        bridges

sudden        grabbing of the ankles

tipping the subject over

the edge

drugs can be very effective

an overdose

of morphine

death without disturbance

two grains will suffice

edge weapons

successfully employed

anatomical knowledge is

puncture wounds

may not

unless the heart is reached

absolute reliability is

severing the spinal cord

with the point of a knife or        light blow

of an axe

## Okay?

> I could stand in the middle of Fifth Avenue
> and shoot somebody and I wouldn't lose
> any voters. Okay? It's like, incredible.
>
> —Donald Trump

I could stand
in the middle of being quoted
as pointing a gun at somebody

in the middle of Fifth Avenue
as saying my feet could stand
in the middle of my skin and shoot somebody

it could be somebody like you
hearing my description of a bullet
making a hole quoted as
splattering blood across Fifth Avenue

across stopped cars and faces of shoppers
standing in the middle of my words

and I wouldn't lose any love
as somebody collapses onto Fifth Avenue

this incredible flower of blood
gushes from the bullet hole
without losing any voters

because this flower says
this microphone grows
my voice goes off-message
into a field of blood flowers like
they're waiting for incredible raindrops

thirsty for my tears
in the middle of quotes about what I could do

what if I get on my knees
beside somebody dying on Fifth Avenue
I could lie down in the middle of my skin

and like press my face
against your very dying face

and cry tears and say I'm sorry
I love you so much
please stay alive
please don't die

and I wouldn't lose

# Eye at the End of a Cape

This looks like a great place for a fort.
The sort of fort that affords more

than one view. Here an ocean, there a bay.
Two observation towers to triangulate

the position of an enemy submarine.
Great place to see without being seen.

A spiral staircase to elevate your head.
There's really no end to the threat.

What if those frothy white waves want
to drown your original thoughts?

What about your online reputation
when out here you get no reception?

No storm's coming, but there is a cloud.
Don't say any true words aloud,

you wrote in a notebook. Once you reveal
your brain, that wound is hard to heal.

That's why this cape curls like a comma
into an ocean of dependent clauses.

Great place to shield you from meaning,
but if someone insists on oversharing

there's really no need to overanalyze.
Talk to your doctor to learn if truth is right

for you. You've come too far not
to live in fear of what bomb could fall

from above. Like a beached horseshoe crab
trying not to die, writhing in the sand,

knowing its ancestors survived extinction.
So much for attachment parenting.

The future eats your fort's meaty walls.
One nation surrounded by saltwater,

under a sunburn god, with SPF 50
for all who are old enough to worry.

Things are dying but not yet dead, like
a botched execution, technically alive

and scanning the horizon for enemies
to make your suffering feel more real.

# Spy vs. Spy Haiku

Can you see eyes that see
you through swirling snowflakes?
Inside winter is a secret winter.

—

Evening lullabies. Icicles
still drip in the last light. A foot
steps into an open manhole.

—

Two spies with dagger faces—
their shadows stretch all afternoon,
almost touching now.

# Drinking

The world's largest online retailer is named after
the world's largest river. At its mouth in Brazil,
the Amazon River can discharge more than
twelve million cubic feet of water per second
into the Atlantic Ocean. At its peak volume,
Amazon.com has sold 636 items per second.

My father didn't live to see the rise of Amazon.com,
but he'd be impressed that so many items can
be purchased at a deep discount without leaving
your home. I can almost hear us talking about it
on the telephone, as if he were still alive.

I might've told him how Amazon.com recommends
items to buy based on past purchases, and how
it has a forum for customer reviews. I might've
told him that today Amazon.com recommended
to me a book of poetry by Rae Armantrout called
*Versed*, winner of the Pulitzer Prize. I clicked on it
and scrolled to the customer reviews. Unfortunately
"Ace 11" gave *Versed* only one out of five stars,
calling it "cocktail coaster jottings" and "obscurity
without purpose." I think there was anger in
Ace 11's tone. Did this anger have a purpose?

Unfortunately my father didn't have much
interest in poetry, but he did like obscurity and
cocktails. His favorite cocktail was a manhattan—
a mix of whiskey, sweet vermouth, and bitters,
often garnished with a maraschino cherry.
He'd often let me eat his maraschino cherry when
I was a kid, and I loved that boozy candy taste.

Over the years my father's drinking increased
and so did his obscurity. He was a frugal man,
so he drank cheap premixed manhattans
by the half-gallon jug. He poured so many
cheap cocktails into his body that he became
too sick and weak to leave his home. Did his
obscurity have a purpose? Probably not.

## The CIA Waterboards KSM at Least 183 Times;
## KSM's Reporting Includes Significant Fabricated Information


On                            was subjected to

ingested a significant amount

of water

"regurgitated gastric acid"

medical officer wrote

"basically doing a series of

near-drownings"

also        insult slap        abdominal slap


efforts to breathe during

holding KSM's lips

directing the water at

exceed the limits

"keeping everyone's butt

out of trouble"

vomited during and after

"seem to have lost ground"

"may poison the well"


despite these reservations        continued for


sleep deprivation        in the standing position

seven-and-a-half days                                "go to school

on this guy"

"next attack on America"


abrasions on his        as well as

hung a picture of

his sons in his cell

a misreading of intelligence

# The New Threat

alien babies watch me through the kitchen window
while I wash dishes listening to talk radio
how many terrorists does it take to stay informed
lately there's been a lot of rain to talk about

explosive puddles have lately filled the alley
and it's nice to have a window to look out there
Mary and Joseph walk by like terrorists in the rain
their eyes look like dishes and their mouths look hungry

I want to fill the sink not with more dirty dishes
but my body and lately I use extra-strength soap
I know terrorists would take my personal information
if they could open this window and crawl into my eyes

but the window is locked and through it I see a baby
lying in a puddle like the rarest meat on a shiny dish
that terrorists have left behind for us to think about
lately I think about that sad baby growing up to be God

lately the kitchen window does a lot of crying
and like terrorists the dishes keep getting dirty

## When I Grew Up

not when I watched the last morphine
sunset drip under your hospital skin

not when I finally forgot being a baby
when my skin grew itchy blooms that

couldn't be scratched enough my fingertips
couldn't squeeze a drop of milk from

my nipples so I learned to hide them
behind complicated polyester shirts

when confessing my dirty little drugs
to the yawning priest I swear to God

it was the Red Scare/mushroom cloud
I swallowed not when you had another

phlegmy coughing fit not when I spied
the whiteness of your bald spot shining

through a bad comb-over from the back seat
of your Ford Pinto with its CIA floor mats

that were really secret compartments
no not even when you called you and all

the other spies living in our white suburb
"spooks" when I learned to hide my pimples

with tinted-for-white-people Clearasil
while trying to stare through the makeup

on the faces of my Kiss album cover
stick a needle in my eye take another

aspirin sky not even when the CIA forced
seven federal prisoners to trip on LSD

for seventy-seven consecutive days
nor when I stepped over a bird's wing

on the sidewalk yesterday and where
was the rest of the body and finally

my body stood on top of the magic word
and off in the distance I could see

some children I think they were
my children yes they were rowing

a slice of bright red birthday cake
beyond the blazing horizon

## Google Street View Haiku

the curtains are open
we watch our eyes on the glowing screen
watching us from the street

zoom in on the ants
crawling over a dead baby bird
lying on the curb

strawberry plants arrived
this morning by FedEx already
I taste their sweet blood

move your cursor where
you want to go then click once
to delete the past

that time pervy Francis Bacon
authored all of Shakespeare's plays
hid secret messages in them

last night I dreamed I was asleep
snoring so loudly my neighbors
plotted to silence me

it's true my loves have all been
suicide kings and drama queens I held
too tightly in my hand

if you remove all the spying
from *Hamlet* "eight unnecessary deaths
could be avoided"

this from a student essay
you can claim to author for free
at www.123helpme.com

now that we see everywhere
our faces lose their high resolution
skin gets blurry

how about I author nothing
and cook myself at 98.6 degrees
for a few centuries LOL!

there must be a god of streets
connecting them all because you can't
see them all at once

thank you for your patience
still on hold with my service provider
ferns waving in the breeze

keep zooming out until
earth is a little ball then a dot
then not even that

## Self-Interrogation

If you swim, yes, you are a swimmer.

If propelling your body through water
with your body, yes. If your body is both vehicle
and what the vehicle carries, yes,

there is water to go through.
There is a problem that swimming wants

to solve: the problem is how to go
through water. To swim, then,

is to solve. Indeed, the swimmer
and solver are one. Or so you hope,

because another problem is fear
of having already swum. Because a swimmer
always wants a little more water

to swim through before arriving.
Yes, you are pathologically late
even though you can describe yourself arriving
on time to dry land. Even though

it's truly possible to say there is a point
at which you no longer swim but have swum.
There is a past participle and yet

pathologically you crave being late.
Because there is so much to do

while swimming. Crying, for example.
There is always so much crying to do,

and when your tears blend with the water
through which you swim, yes,
it feels like the problem has just arrived

even though it happened in fourth grade.
You can actually describe yourself
in fourth grade chewing on a pen
because you were so nervous,

and of course the pen broke in your mouth
and your mouth turned black with ink.
Your lips turned black, and some ink
trickled down your chin. And only

now in the lateness of being there
can you see how other kids saw so clearly
what happened, your face cracking open,

your body trying to swim through water
to wash off the ink, your body

swimming toward the shore of having swum.

Yes, you still have not finished swimming.
It is safer not to finish anything.

You don't want to die having
finished anything.

# Notes

"House of Helicopters": epigraph from Sarah Fox's "Essay on My Memory," published in *The First Flag* (Minneapolis: Coffee House Press, 2013).

"A State of Permanent Visibility": epigraph from "Panopticism," from Michel Foucault's *Discipline & Punish,* trans. Alan Sheridan (New York: Vintage Books, 1977), p. 207.

"CIA Training Manual: Interrogation": all words taken from the CIA training manual "KUBARK Counterintelligence Interrogation," July 1963, Document 1A, pp. 65–66. Released in "Prisoner Abuse: Patterns from the Past," *National Security Archive Electronic Briefing Book No. 122* (http://www2 .gwu.edu/~nsarchiv/NSAEBB/NSAEBB122).

"CIA Training Manual: The Art of Deception": all words taken from "Some Operational Applications of the Art of Deception," a CIA training manual written by well-known magician, John Mulholland, 1953, pp. 77–83, published in *The Official C.I.A. Manual of Trickery and Deception,* by H. Keith Melton and Robert Wallace (New York: Harper Collins, 2009).

"CIA Training Manual: Theory of Coercion": all words taken from the CIA training manual "KUBARK Counterintelligence Interrogation," July 1963, Document 1B, pp. 82–85. Released in "Prisoner Abuse: Patterns from the Past," *National Security Archive Electronic Briefing Book No. 122* (http://www2 .gwu.edu/~nsarchiv/NSAEBB/NSAEBB122).

"Coin Toss at Dusk": epigraph from "I Just Realized," by Valerie Mejer Caso, trans. Torin Jensen, published in *Make X: A Decade of Literary Art,* eds. Daniel Borzutzky et al. (Chicago: Featherproof Books, 2016).

"CIA Training Manual: Non-coercive Interrogation Techniques": all words taken from the CIA training manual "KUBARK Counterintelligence Interrogation," July 1963, Document 1A, pp. 66–81. Released in "Prisoner Abuse: Patterns from the Past," *National Security Archive Electronic Briefing Book No. 122* (http://www2.gwu.edu/~nsarchiv/NSAEBB/NSAEBB122).

"CIA Museum": all words taken from the CIA Museum's online collection of historical artifacts, "Experience the Collection," located on the website of the CIA (https://www.cia.gov/about-cia/cia-museum/experience-the-collection /#!/collection/show-all).

"Overthrow Install": adapted from "A Timeline of CIA Atrocities," by Steve Kangas, on Global Research, the website of the Centre for Research on Globalization (http://www.globalresearch.ca/a-timeline-of-cia-atrocities /5348804), and *Rogue State: A Guide to the World's Only Superpower,* 3rd ed., by William Blum (Monroe, ME: Common Courage Press, 2000).

"Safe Houses I Have Known": epigraph from *Tinker Tailor Soldier Spy,* by John le Carré (London: Paperview, 2004), pp. 264–65, which was originally published in 1974. I discovered this passage containing the phrase "safe houses I have known" many years after my father died and many years after he told me that if he ever wrote a memoir about his spy experiences, this phrase would be its title. I do know that *Tinker Tailor Soldier Spy* was one of his favorite books, but I don't know if he was aware of borrowing the phrase or if he did so unintentionally.

"CIA Training Manual: A Study of Assassination": all words taken from a CIA training manual related to the 1954 coup in Guatemala, excerpted by William Blum in *Rogue State,* pp. 56–57.

"The CIA Waterboards KSM at Least 183 Times; KSM's Reporting Includes Significant Fabricated Information": all words taken from the U.S. Senate report "Committee Study of the Central Intelligence Agency's Detention and Interrogation Program," 2014, pp. 85–91 (http://upload.wikimedia .org/wikipedia/commons/a/a2/US_Senate_Report_on_CIA_Detention_ Interrogation_Program.pdf).

A number of poems in this book were informed by Tim Weiner's work in *Legacy of Ashes: The History of the CIA* (New York: Anchor Books, 2008).

# Acknowledgments

Thanks infinitely and eternally to my amazing spouse, best friend, and first editor, Jessica Knight. So grateful for all the time, intelligence, and vision you've given these poems.

Thanks to my kids, Nico and Ramona, for love, laughter, and inspiring weirdness.

Thanks to Randall Heath, Sarah Fox, and Kevin Carollo for all the creative collaboration that helped hatch many of these poems.

Thanks to everyone who read and offered feedback to early versions of this book, including Eric Lorberer, Paula Cisewski, and Sarah Fox.

Thanks to the editors of the following magazines in which many of these poems were previously published: *Boston Review;* the *Boog Reader; Columbia Poetry Review; Denver Quarterly; Forklift, Ohio; Indiana Review; jubilat;* the *Literary Review; Make;* the *Nation; Poetry City, USA; Revolver;* the *Third Rail;* and *Volt.*

Thanks to Kevin A. Gonzalez and Lauren Shapiro for including "Rearview" (with a different title) and two other poems of mine in *The New Census: An Anthology of Contemporary American Poetry.*

Thanks to Kelly Everding and Eric Lorberer of *Rain Taxi Review of Books,* who first published "Surveillance Video of a Bridge" (with a different title) in a chapbook called *Bridge: A Gathering,* in honor of the fifth anniversary of the I-35W bridge collapse in Minneapolis.

Thanks to all those who help make the Minneapolis/St. Paul poetry community so vibrant and nurturing, including William Waltz, Dobby Gibson, Matt Mauch, Mary Austin Speaker, Chris Martin, Tish Jones, Kathryn Kysar, Betsy Brown, Ed Bok Lee, KateLynn Hibbard, Valérie Déus, Morgan Willow, Greg Hewett, Sun Yung Shin, G. E. Patterson, Rachel Moritz, Matt Rasmussen, Patrick Werle, Luke Pingel, Elisabeth Workman, and Douglas Kearney.

Thanks to everyone at Coffee House Press for believing in this book and for promoting the social mission of literature, including Chris Fischbach, Erika Stevens, Lizzie Davis, Carla Valadez, and Jay Peterson.

This book was written while listening to the music of William Basinski, Federico Durand, Hakobune, Wil Bolton, Chihei Hatakeyama, Sarah Davachi, Christopher Bissonnette, Nobuto Suda, Kyle Bobby Dunn, Marcus Fischer, Pausal, Christopher Hipgrave, Simon Bainton, Rafael Anton Irisarri, Taylor Deupree, willamette, Tomasz Bednarczyk.

LITERATURE
is not the same thing as
PUBLISHING

Coffee House Press began as a small letterpress operation in 1972 and has grown into an internationally renowned nonprofit publisher of literary fiction, essay, poetry, and other work that doesn't fit neatly into genre categories.

Coffee House is both a publisher and an arts organization. Through our *Books in Action* program and publications, we've become interdisciplinary collaborators and incubators for new work and audience experiences. Our vision for the future is one where a publisher is a catalyst and connector.

# Funder Acknowledgments

Coffee House Press is an internationally renowned independent book publisher and arts nonprofit based in Minneapolis, MN; through its literary publications and *Books in Action* program, Coffee House acts as a catalyst and connector—between authors and readers, ideas and resources, creativity and community, inspiration and action.

Coffee House Press books are made possible through the generous support of grants and donations from corporations, state and federal grant programs, family foundations, and the many individuals who believe in the transformational power of literature. This activity is made possible by the voters of Minnesota through a Minnesota State Arts Board Operating Support grant, thanks to the legislative appropriation from the Arts and Cultural Heritage Fund. Coffee House also receives major operating support from the Amazon Literary Partnership, Jerome Foundation, McKnight Foundation, Target Foundation, and the National Endowment for the Arts (NEA). To find out more about how NEA grants impact individuals and communities, visit www.arts.gov.

Coffee House Press receives additional support from the Elmer L. & Eleanor J. Andersen Foundation; the David & Mary Anderson Family Foundation; Bookmobile; Dorsey & Whitney LLP; Foundation Technologies; Fredrikson & Byron, P.A.; the Fringe Foundation; Kenneth Koch Literary Estate; the Matching Grant Program Fund of the Minneapolis Foundation; Mr. Pancks' Fund in memory of Graham Kimpton; the Schwab Charitable Fund; Schwegman, Lundberg & Woessner, P.A.; the Silicon Valley Community Foundation; and the U.S. Bank Foundation.

# The Publisher's Circle of Coffee House Press

Publisher's Circle members make significant contributions to Coffee House Press's annual giving campaign. Understanding that a strong financial base is necessary for the press to meet the challenges and opportunities that arise each year, this group plays a crucial part in the success of Coffee House's mission.

Recent Publisher's Circle members include many anonymous donors, Suzanne Allen, Patricia A. Beithon, the E. Thomas Binger & Rebecca Rand Fund of the Minneapolis Foundation, Andrew Brantingham, Robert & Gail Buuck, Dave & Kelli Cloutier, Louise Copeland, Jane Dalrymple-Hollo & Stephen Parlato, Mary Ebert & Paul Stembler, Kaywin Feldman & Jim Lutz, Chris Fischbach & Katie Dublinski, Sally French, Jocelyn Hale & Glenn Miller, the Rehael Fund-Roger Hale/Nor Hall of the Minneapolis Foundation, Randy Hartten & Ron Lotz, Dylan Hicks & Nina Hale, William Hardacker, Randall Heath, Jeffrey Hom, Carl & Heidi Horsch, the Amy L. Hubbard & Geoffrey J. Kehoe Fund, Kenneth & Susan Kahn, Stephen & Isabel Keating, Julia Klein, the Kenneth Koch Literary Estate, Cinda Kornblum, Jennifer Kwon Dobbs & Stefan Liess, the Lambert Family Foundation, the Lenfestey Family Foundation, Joy Linsday Crow, Sarah Lutman & Rob Rudolph, the Carol & Aaron Mack Charitable Fund of the Minneapolis Foundation, George & Olga Mack, Joshua Mack & Ron Warren, Gillian McCain, Malcolm S. McDermid & Katie Windle, Mary & Malcolm McDermid, Sjur Midness & Briar Andresen, Maureen Millea Smith & Daniel Smith, Peter Nelson & Jennifer Swenson, Enrique & Jennifer Olivarez, Alan Polsky, Marc Porter & James Hennessy, Robin Preble, Alexis Scott, Ruth Stricker Dayton, Jeffrey Sugerman & Sarah Schultz, Nan G. & Stephen C. Swid, Kenneth Thorp in memory of Allan Kornblum & Rochelle Ratner, Patricia Tilton, Joanne Von Blon, Stu Wilson & Melissa Barker, Warren D. Woessner & Iris C. Freeman, and Margaret Wurtele.

For more information about the Publisher's Circle and other ways to support Coffee House Press books, authors, and activities, please visit www.coffeehousepress.org/pages/support or contact us at info@coffeehousepress.org.

**Steve Healey** is the author of two previous books of poetry, *10 Mississippi* and *Earthling,* both from Coffee House Press. His poems have been published in magazines such as the *American Poetry Review, Boston Review, Denver Quarterly, Fence, jubilat,* and the *Nation,* and in anthologies, most recently *The New Census: An Anthology of Contemporary American Poetry.* He's a professor of English and creative writing at Minneapolis College.

*Safe Houses I Have Known* was designed by
Bookmobile Design & Digital Publisher Services.
Text is set in Legacy Serif ITC.